Published by **Lion Cub Books**

www.spck.org.uk

Part of the SPCK Group

Studio 101, The Record Hall, 16-16A Baldwin's Gardens, EC1N 7RJ

ISBN 978-1915748-26-3

First edition 2023

First US edition 2025

A catalogue record for this book is available from the British Library

Produced on paper from sustainable sources

Printed and bound in China by Dream Colour (Hong Kong) Printing Ltd

Share a Story
BIBLE
Buddies

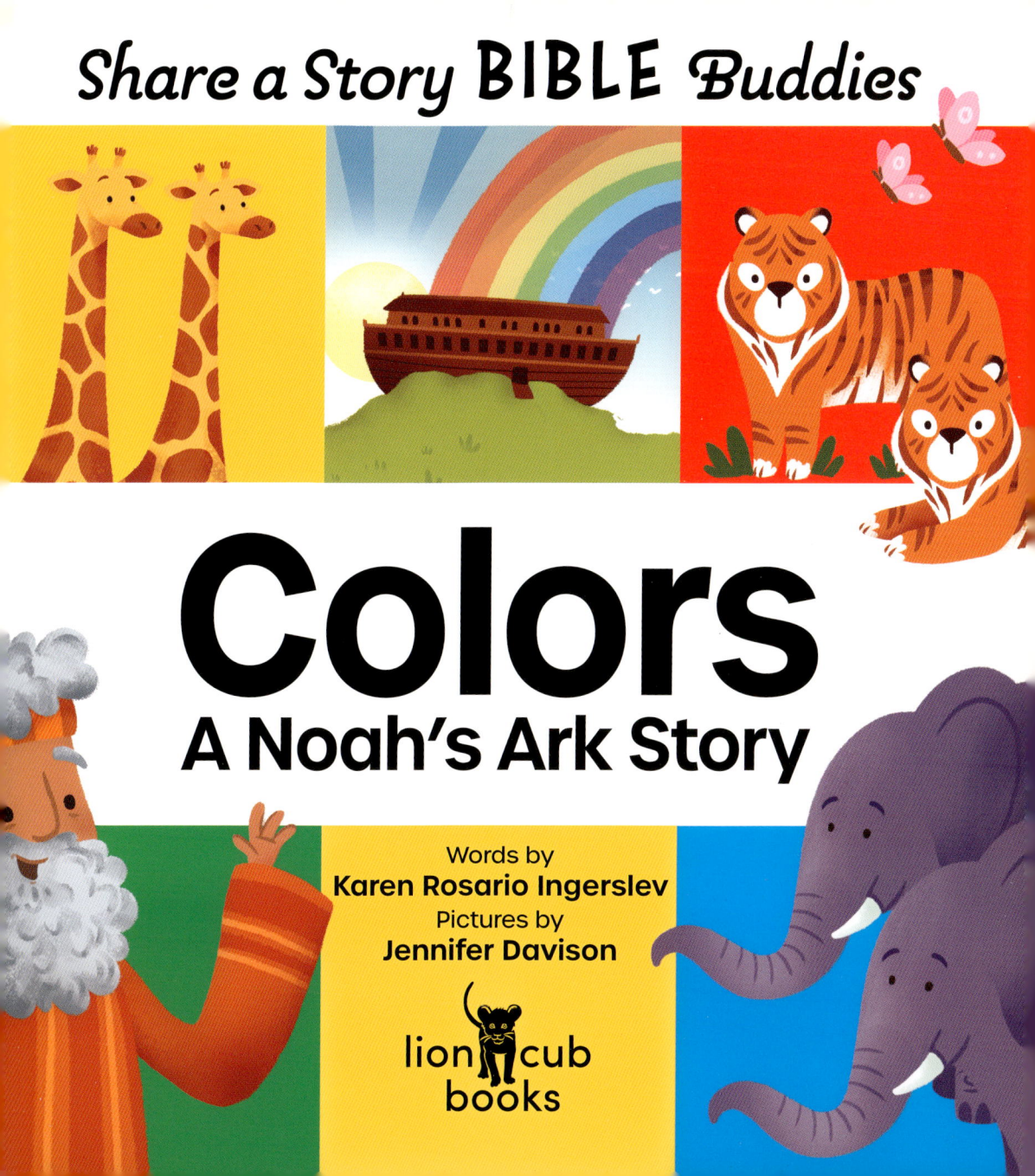

Share a Story **BIBLE** Buddies

Colors
A Noah's Ark Story

Words by
Karen Rosario Ingerslev
Pictures by
Jennifer Davison

lion cub
books

brown

Noah built
a big brown boat.

black

He used black tar so it would float.

red

In slither
two red snakes.

purple

The purple chameleons are wide awake.

green

Two green frogs
do funny jumps.

orange

The orange camels have big humps.

yellow

Hear the yellow lions roar.

pink

Two pink
butterflies
at the door.

gray

The gray clouds burst, the rain begins.

gray

blue

Blue water covers everything.

blue

white

The pure white dove is flying high.

white

rainbow

See the rainbow in the sky!

red

orange

yellow

green

blue

indigo

violet

rainbow

brown

black

red

purple

green

orange

yellow

pink

gray

blue

white

ALSO IN THE

Share a Story **BIBLE** *Buddies*

SERIES

Numbers: A Nativity Story

ISBN 978-0-7459-9801-5